Famous American Women

Gregory Guiteras

Dover Publications, Inc.
Mineola, New York

In memory of my parents,
Virginia Kline Guiteras
and George Gustavo Guiteras
—GREGORY GUITERAS

In memory of Bertha Sussman Scheib
(also known as "Grandma Bertie"),
and in honor of Esther Frank Smith,
women with lifetimes of caring and daring
—THE EDITOR

Bibliographical Note

Famous American Women is a new work, first published by Dover Publications, Inc., in 2001.

DOVER *Pictorial Archive* SERIES

International Standard Book Number: 0-486-41548-1

Manufactured in the United States of America
Dover Publications, Inc., 31 East 2nd Street, Mineola, N.Y. 11501

Introduction

Although no effort was made to match any other list of women widely considered to be outstanding, influential, or just plain famous, it happens that of the 45 women portrayed in this book, 25 were among the "100 Most Influential Women in World History" chosen by an editor in 1995, with input from dozens of U.S. professors of women's studies.

The women introduced in the pages of this book made outstanding contributions in a multitude of fields, from anthropology to astronomy, from Congress to cooking, from sculpture to social work, from nail polish to nursing. Despite their varied activities, they all have some things in common. Foremost among their shared traits, perhaps, are: caring passionately about something; remarkable energy; daring to be first, best, or alone in an endeavor; and tenacity to keep on trying when others give in to discouragement. It is interesting to see how many of these strongly motivated women not only lived to be more than 80 years old, or even more than 90, but still were active in their chosen work almost until the end of their life.

Some of these women sought to express themselves creatively, through painting, sculpture, music, or dance. Others were determined to change society for the better, by means of political action, social work, community organizing, or public health services. Some were outstandingly successful in business, by means of inventivenesss and willingness to take risks. None defined success merely as power to dictate to other people. Most of them showed great courage or compassion, or both, as they tried to reach their goals, to make their dreams realities. Quite a few of them nurtured several children—some as single mothers—while making their mark in the world in more public ways. Others chose not to marry or have children, or felt that they did not have that option, if they were to reach their goals beyond the sphere of home and family.

Some seemed full of contradictions, even to people who knew them well (Emma Goldman and Isadora Duncan come to mind). If we could examine the lives of a similar number of *not-famous* women who have made and are making remarkable contributions to society, we would notice the same variety of responses to the world that we see when we compare these famous outstanding women, or even when we look at different phases of each woman's life. This shows that what poet Judy Grahn wrote is true: "The common woman is as common as a common loaf of bread." Just as every loaf of bread is *un*common, having its own size, form, texture, aroma, and flavor, every woman, famous or not, is uncommon—in fact, unique.

When we begin to know the environments, the experiences, the motives, the hopes and fears, the joys and disappointments of a few women who are admired by many people, we learn about making choices—and about "making lemonade" when life hands us lemons. We may begin to see the greatness in "everyday" women we know. We may get some ideas about our own potential to be and do.

None of these women was born great. Many of them did not really get going at what became their life's work until they were past 30, 40, or 50. Eleanor Roosevelt, thought by many to be the greatest woman of the 20th century, recalled late in life, "It was not until I reached middle age that I had the courage to develop interests of my own." Margaret Chase Smith, who was 43 when she was elected to the U.S. House of Representatives to "take her husband's place" after he died, had four books in progress, including a novel about the U.S. Senate, when she died at age 98.

Many of the women portrayed in this book have written about their own lives. Here is a sampling of such book-length accounts that can be found in many public libraries: Marian Anderson, *My Lord, What a Morning;* Maya Angelou, *I Know Why the Caged Bird Sings;* Brooke Astor, *A Patchwork Childhood* and *Footprints;* Margaret Bourke-White, *Portrait of Myself;* Isadora Duncan, *My Life;* Emma Goldman, *Living My Life;* Zora Neale Hurston, *Dust Tracks on a Road;* Helen Keller, *The Story of My Life;* Margaret Mead, *Blackberry Winter;* Mary Pickford, *Sunshine and Shadows;* Eleanor Roosevelt, *This I Remember;* Margaret Sanger, *Margaret Sanger;* Harriet Tubman, *Harriet Tubman, The Moses of Her People* (as told to Sarah Bradford); Edith Wharton, *A Backwards Glance.* In addition, chapters on many of these women are included in various collections of biographies, and some of the women have had several books for children and teenagers written about them. In *Particular Passions,* capsule biographies and portrait photos of dozens of outstanding U.S. women are presented along with the women's own words when they were interviewed for the book. Friedan, Mead, Nevelson, Vreeland, and Walters are included. In *American Women: Their Lives in Their Words,* Doreen Rappaport writes about the challenges met and feats accomplished by dozens of women—some famous and others not—at various times and in several regions, during more than 200 years of U.S. history. Each woman is represented by a passage from her writing: letters, diaries, speeches, essays. Among the voices heard are Blackwell, Mead, Roosevelt, Sanger, and Stanton.

Chronological Life-and-Work Index

As a child, **Madeleine Albright** (1937–) lived in Nazi-occupied Czechoslovakia during World War II. In 1948, with the Soviet Union in power there, her family received political asylum in the United States. She was fluent in five languages when she finished college. Marrying a newspaper heir, she earned an M.A. and a Ph.D. in Russian history at Columbia University while raising three daughters. In Washington, D.C., she joined the National Security Council staff, divorced in 1980, taught International Affairs at Georgetown University, and was at the Center for National Policy. In 1993 President Clinton appointed her as U.S. representative to the United Nations. He chose her in 1996 as the first woman Secretary of State.

Alto **Marian Anderson** (1897–1993), her sisters, and their mother barely scraped by after her father died young. People at her family's Baptist church raised funds for singing lessons for her. A 1925 competition in New York led to studies and concerts in Europe, and she sold out Carnegie Hall in 1936. When she sang at the Lincoln Memorial on Easter Sunday in 1939 (arranged by Eleanor Roosevelt after a major concert hall was refused to a "Negro"), 75,000 people were present. About prejudice she said, "You lose a lot of time hating people." In 1955, when she was nearly 60, she sang in *Un Ballo in Maschera* at the Metropolitan Opera and became U.S. delegate to the United Nations.

Maya Angelou (1928–) was so abused in her early childhood that she was unable to speak for five years. Other harsh experiences followed when she and her brother lived in rural Arkansas with their grandmother after their parents separated. She later said, "Children's talent to endure stems from their ignorance of alternatives." Somehow freeing her voice, she expressed herself fully as a singer, dancer, actress, public speaker, prolific writer of memoirs, and poet. Fame followed publication of *I Know Why the Caged Bird Sings,* the first of four books she wrote about her life. She lived in Africa for a time and is the mother of a son. Named professor of American Studies at Wake Forest University, N.C., she has traveled widely, speaking to people of all ages.

Susan B. Anthony (1820–1906) a Quaker teacher, right, began her feminist career in 1853 at the New York State Teachers Association annual meeting, as the first woman to make public comments at the gathering. In 1872, after she and her sisters registered to vote in Rochester, N.Y., 50 women did the same. She voted, but was arrested and prevented from bringing the case to the Supreme Court. At 84, she founded the International Women's Suffrage Association. Her terse slogan was: "Men, their rights and nothing more; women, their rights and nothing less." Her friend **Elizabeth Cady Stanton** (1815–1902) did not promise to obey her husband, when she married in 1840. The fond mother of seven children, she organized the Seneca Falls Convention in 1848, launching the U.S. struggle for women's rights. She wrote, "Here's to the mothers . . . with restless children in migrant wagons, cooking meals by day, nursing babies by night, while the men slept." In 1869 she founded the National Women's Suffrage Association with Anthony. A fine orator, she traveled less than unmarried, childless Anthony.

Brooke Astor (1902–), the well-traveled only child of a career marine officer, was bereft when her second husband died. When in 1959 her third husband, heir to John Jacob Astor's fortune, left a foundation with $57 million in assets "for the alleviation of human misery," she began giving away money—more than $200 million in all—remarkably visiting "everyone" among the recipient organizations, which prominently include The New York Public Library. The author of two memoirs, *A Patchwork Childhood* (1962) and *Footprints* (1980) and two novels (1965 and 1986), she also writes poetry. She muses, "Women now have so many resources. . . . [W]e only had one: we flirted."

Clara Barton (1821–1912), her farmer parents' "late child," had no playmates. After nursing a severely ill older brother for two years, at 15 she began teaching. Later living in Washington, D.C., when the Civil War began, she collected supplies on her own and took them to Union soldiers, mid-1862 through 1864. In Europe to recover from nervous disorders after more war-related tasks, she instead plunged into Franco-Prussian War relief work. Her five-year lone effort got the American Red Cross authorized, and she then won international support for peacetime disaster relief. In 1900 this tiny, willful woman, 79, personally aided Galveston flood victims. Her motto: "Everybody's business is nobody's business . . . is my business."

Amy Beach (1867–1944) debuted as a concert pianist in 1884 and married Dr. Henry Beach, who encouraged her to compose. Two years later, the Boston Symphony premiered her "Gaelic" symphony. In 1892 she became the first woman whose work was performed by the New York Philharmonic Society. Her piano concerto was premiered in Boston in 1900. After her husband's death in 1910, she toured Europe giving concerts until World War I began. Her symphony was performed in Berlin and Leipzig. An opera, *Cabildo* (1932), was among her more than 150 works. She was a founder and the first president (1926) of the Association of American Women Composers.

Elizabeth Blackwell (1821–1910) was born in England and lived there after 1869, but is honored as the first U.S. woman to become a medical doctor. A teacher, she was rejected by 28 medical schools, then accepted at Geneva Medical College in 1847 when the students voted her in as a joke. She was seriously harassed there, but wrote in her journal, "The little fat Professor of Anatomy is a capital fellow; . . . I shall love fat men more than lean ones henceforth." After graduating she worked in Paris and London hospitals. In 1851 she moved to New York City's slums to serve the poor, commenting once, "I *should* like a little fun now and then." She founded the New York Infirmary for Women and Children in 1857, working with her younger sister, Emily, and Polish physician Marie Zakrzewska, and in 1866 added the Women's Medical College.

Margaret Bourke-White (1904–1971) always knew "I had to travel. I pictured myself doing all the things that women never do." She married while at one of seven colleges she attended, but her mother-in-law soon soured the match. "I chose Cornell [from which she graduated] not for its zoology courses but because . . . there were waterfalls on campus," she later said. Her striking photos of industrial Cleveland won acclaim. Hired by the new *Fortune* magazine in 1929, she saw the human effects of the 1934 Midwest drought. In 1936 she did *Life*'s first cover-story photos. She and writer Erskine Caldwell ("Skinny") created the book *You Have Seen Their Faces*, which portrayed poor southern farm people during the Depression, and were married briefly. Her World War II Army Air Force photos ended with "The Living Dead of Buchenwald" set, taken when the concentration camp was liberated.

Rachel Carson (1907–1964) loved writing and nature (at ten, she had a story published in *St. Nicholas* children's magazine). She majored in English, then biology, and earned an M.A. in genetics. As a federal Fisheries biologist, she produced superb booklets on wildlife refuges. A 1937 *Atlantic Monthly* article grew into her 1941 book *Under the Sea Wind*. "No one could write truly about the sea and leave out the poetry," she noted. *The Sea Around Us* (1951) was a bestseller. In 1955, living in Maine, she wrote *The Edge of the Sea*. A guide for helping children know and love nature, *The Sense of Wonder*, was inspired by her great-nephew, five. Bone cancer was ending her life when her pesticide warning, *Silent Spring*, made ecology vital.

Mary Cassatt (1844–1926) studied art in Philadelphia during the Civil War. In Europe she viewed works by Correggio, Velásquez, Rubens, and Hals. In 1872 she became obsessed with a Degas pastel she saw in a Paris display window. She met the artist when he admired her *Portrait d'Ida* at the 1874 Salon. Both exhibited with the Impressionists 1877–1881, and again in 1886. Her work included oils, drawings, pastels, and water-colors. Cassatt's subjects usually were women's daily activities, and mothers with children. After viewing Japanese prints in 1890, she began making prints with metal plates. Glimpsing the abstract art of Picasso and Matisse on Gertrude Stein's walls in 1908, when her vision was impaired, she said, "I want to be taken home at once."

Willa Cather (1873–1947) was taken from Virginia's wooded Shenandoah Valley to barren-seeming Nebraska as a child. "Sodbusters," many of them European immigrants, were making prairie farms. After college she worked as a journalist. Her 1905 book of stories, *The Troll Garden*, won her a job at *McClure's* monthly in New York. Her novels, such as *O Pioneers!* (1913), *My Ántonia* (1918), and *Death Comes for* the *Archbishop* (1927), celebrated the "American spirit" triumphing over hardship. *One of Ours* (1922) won her a Pulitzer prize. *Sapphira and the Slave Girl* (1940) depicted early Virginia settlers. World War I changed her world greatly. She said, "The dead might as well try to speak to the living as the old to the young."

Eileen Collins (1956-) earned a bachelor's degree at Syracuse University, after studies in math, science, and economics. Commissioned a second lieutenant in 1978, she soon graduated from U.S. Air Force undergraduate pilot training. In the 1980s she earned two master's degrees (in Operations Research and in Space Systems Management), married, completed test-pilot school, commanded an aircraft, and taught mathematics at the USAF Academy. She became a National Aeronautics and Space Administration (NASA) astronaut in 1990 and a lieutenant colonel in 1993. Second-in-command of the space shuttle *Discovery* in 1995 and the *Atlantis* in 1997 (the first woman to pilot a shuttle), in March 1999 she commanded the *Columbia*.

13

Emily Dickinson (1830–1886) had an autocratic father who let her attend Mt. Holyoke Female Seminary, but apart from one visit apiece to Washington, D.C., Philadelphia, and Boston, she never left her hometown, Amherst, Massachusetts, after that. A recluse who always dressed in white, she wrote her short poems on scraps of paper. Poet and abolitionist Thomas Wentworth Higginson did not appreciate her work when she asked him to comment on it in 1862, but in the 1890s he coedited her poetry in three volumes. Her sister had saved more than 1,700 poems left at Emily's death, instead of burning them as Emily wanted.

Isadora Duncan (1877–1927) was a vagabond during her childhood and youth with her permissive music-teacher mother and three siblings. A "natural" dancer, she created modern dance, blending poetry, melody, and movement—as Edith Wharton wrote, "an endless interweaving . . . satisfying every sense." Mingling with artists and writers in London and Paris by 1900, she triumphed in Berlin, Budapest, and Bayreuth, but broke contracts when lovestruck, rejected classical ballet, and said "America knows nothing of food, love, or art." In 1913 her children, 6 and 3, drowned in the Seine river in a runaway car. She had one good U.S. tour with conductor Walter Damrosch's orchestra, but her 1922–23 tour was a fiasco. Four years later, she was killed when her shawl caught in a sportscar's wheel and broke her neck during a test drive.

Amelia Earhart (1897–1937) was a military nurse in Canada during World War I and then a social worker. In 1931, already a pilot, she wrote to publisher G. P. Putnam, on their wedding eve: "I cannot guarantee to endure . . . the confinements of even an attractive cage." She made a solo Atlantic flight in 1932, and flew Hawaii to California in 1935. After a 1933 White House dinner, she piloted Eleanor Roosevelt on a thrilling night flight (in evening gowns), then "ER" gave her a joyride in a brand-new White House car. The aviator wrote that she knew "girls who should be tinkering with mechanical things instead of making dresses and boys who would do better at cooking. . . . Girls . . . whose tastes aren't routine often don't get a fair break." Earhart disappeared during a planned trans-Pacific flight in 1937. Her fate is unknown.

Fannie Farmer (1857–1915) was going to attend college despite her family's modest means, but a stroke paralyzed her left leg when she was 16. She was 30 when she began two years of study at the Boston Cooking School. Made assistant to the director, she was chosen as director in 1891. Her Boston Cooking School Cook Book (1896) pioneered the use of clear instructions, with exact measurements and timing. Shy Ms. Farmer shunned publicity as the book went through 21 editions. In 1902 she founded Miss Farmer's School of Cookery. Teaching nutrition and working with Harvard Medical School, she wrote a book on cooking for sick and convalescent people, and four other cookbooks.

Betty Friedan (1921–), born in Peoria, Illinois, graduated *summa cum laude* as a psychology student and won a coveted fellowship (she turned it down, as a potential husband was wary of such attainments). After years of a 1950s European-American, middle-class, suburban existence, in 1963 she published *The Feminine Mystique*. The book touched a nerve and was credited with sparking a new feminism. Said its combative, intellectual author, "This movement had to do with . . . life in the kitchen, the bedroom, . . . the office." The first president of the National Organization for Women (1966–1970) divorced in 1969. Twelve years later, she published *The Second Wave*. It seemed reformist rather than radical, to some.

Emma Goldman (1869–1940) had a harsh childhood in Russia. Sewing in factories ruined her eyesight. At 20 she took a sewing machine and $5 to New York City. Called a menace after her beloved Alexander Berkman tried to kill an industrialist hated by workers, she was said by journalist H. L. Mencken to preach simply the Beatitudes. She studied nursing in Vienna and opened an ice-cream parlor with Berkman when he was out of prison. A great speaker (in four languages) on social issues, she also published *Mother Earth* for 12 years. Deported to Russia in 1919, she reported the new Soviet Union's faults. By 1927 fighting injustice seemed futile, but she went on. Never grim about life, she said: "If I can't dance, I don't want your revolution."

After college, **Katharine Meyer Graham** (1917–) reported for the *Washington Post,* owned by her father. Her husband, Philip, became president after World War II. In 1961 *Newsweek* was acquired. Two years later, when Phil killed himself, "Kay" took over as president until a son could handle the job. Instead, by 1973 she was board chairperson, CEO, and publisher—allow-ing full editorial freedom. She gave funds to help start *Ms.* magazine in 1971. *Washington Post* reporters exposed the Watergate scandal. Honored in 1974 as "the most powerful woman in America," she quipped that this sounded like "female weightlifter." In 1997 she wrote, "To love what you do and feel that it matters—how could anything be more fun?"

Karen Horney (1885–1952), born in Germany, studied medicine despite her father's disapproval, married in 1909, and had three daughters before earning the M.D. degree at 30. After World War I she specialized at the Berlin Psychoanalytic Institute. In 1932, no longer married, she moved to New York. Her books *The Neurotic Personality of Our Time* (1937) and *New*

Ways in Psychoanalysis (1939) broke new ground. She founded an association for and an institute of psychoanalysis, and edited the *American Journal of Psychoanalysis*. A feminist who cogently challenged Freud, she noted, "Fortunately analysis is not the only way to resolve inner conflicts. Life itself remains a very effective therapist."

Zora Neale Hurston (1903–1960) grew up in an African-American town in Florida where her father was mayor for a time. Her mother told her, "Jump at de sun!" to get off the ground. After studies with anthropologist Franz Boas, she did ethnographic work in Haiti and the United States. During the Harlem Renaissance, she wrote, "I am not tragically colored. . . .—I am too busy sharpening my oyster knife." Of photos of herself, she said, "I love myself when I'm laughing, and then again when I am looking mean and impressive." Hurston published novels, short stories, essays, and plays, as well as an autobiography, *Dust Tracks on a Road*, but she is best known for her writings on African-American folklore and culture in the United States and in Haiti (*Mules and Men, Tell My Horse*) and for her 1937 novel *Their Eyes Were Watching God*, which depicts a strong African-American woman who is both loving and self-respecting in her relationships. Hurston wrote the play *Mulebone* with Langston Hughes. Nearly a dozen of her unpublished plays were found in the 1990s. She spent her last decade in poverty, working as a librarian in Florida part of the time. She was semiforgotten until novelist Alice Walker spotlighted her life and work in the 1970s.

Helen Keller (1880–1968), blind and deaf after a babyhood illness, could not speak intelligibly. Anne Sullivan, a visually impaired graduate of the Perkins School for the Blind, arrived at her family's Georgia home in 1887, shortly before Helen's seventh birthday. Sullivan had been hired to try to teach the "unreachable" child, who had lost even basic abilities developed as a baby. So seemingly miraculous was the progress they made that Helen, accompanied by Anne, earned a college degree in 1904. Two years earlier, *The Story of My Life* had been published. Helen had a full life as a lecturer and writer. Among her published opinions was "... the day that militarism is undermined, capitalism will fail."

Barbara McClintock (1902–1992) was taken to Brooklyn at age 6 and graduated from intellectually challenging Erasmus Hall High School at 16. She earned a B.Sc., M.A., and Ph.D. at Cornell College of Agriculture by 1927 and coauthored a pioneering paper on maize chromosomes in 1931. After giving up a Guggenheim Fellowship in Nazi Germany, she began genetic research at Cold Spring Harbor Laboratory and made the crucial discovery that chromosomes are not stable: genes change unpredictably over generations. She was president of the Genetics Society in 1944, but her findings were ignored or derided for decades. She still was active in 1983 when her immense contribution to genetics was recognized with the Nobel Prize for Medicine and Physiology.

Margaret Mead (1901–1978) radically changed our understanding of the effects of nature and nurture on gender roles. She studied with cultural anthropologist Franz Boas, then earned an M.A. in psychology. As field researcher, curator, and professor, she was associated with the American Museum of Natural History and with Columbia University for more than 50 years. Some of the most notable among her more than 40 books were *Coming of Age in Samoa* (1928), *Growing Up in New Guinea* (1930), *Sex and Temperament in Three Primitive Societies* (1935), and *Male and Female* (1949). She measured success by "the contributions an individual makes to her or his fellow human beings," she stated.

Maria Mitchell (1818–1889), born on Nantucket island, was one of ten children of Quaker parents. As a child, she helped her father, who was an amateur astronomer, to observe and calculate. Attracted by mathematics, she read LaPlace, Gauss in Latin, and other advanced treatises when she worked as librarian at the local Atheneum. In 1847, using an old telescope, she discovered a new comet. This brought her fame and a fine new instrument, a gift from U.S. women admirers. In 1861 she became professor of astronomy at the new Vassar College. Her reputation gave the institution prestige. A witty, kindly teacher, she promoted higher education for women.

Toni Morrison (1931–), born in industrial Lorain, Ohio, taught at Howard University, then moved to New York City in 1965. She was one of the first African-American editors for a major book publisher, and was the mother of two sons before she became a full-time fiction writer. *The Bluest Eye* (1970), *Song of Solomon* (1977), and *Tar Baby* (1981) riveted readers. *Beloved* earned a Pulitzer prize in 1988. Her books matter-of-factly depict extreme cruelty and violence. She was teaching at Princeton in 1993 when she was awarded the Nobel Prize in Literature, published *Jazz,* and returned to editing. A 1998 novel, *Paradise,* portrayed the remaining residents in a once-thriving African-American town in Kansas.

Ukraine-born **Louise Nevelson** (1900–1988) grew up in Maine, studying voice, acting, dancing, and playing basketball. Marrying a shipbuilding heir when she finished high school, she lived in New York City in high style. After studies at the Art Students' League and with architect Hans Hofmann in Vienna, she divorced and in 1932 assisted Mexican muralist Diego Rivera. Nevelson was known for sculptures that enclosed space with carved pieces and found objects (painted black or white). Later she made large metal and Plexiglas® pieces, sculpting "to see the world with more awareness and more harmony." In the 1930s she had some success, but at times she was depressed. When people asked, "Aren't you glad you were born?" she would retort, "If I wasn't I wouldn't know the difference."

Sandra Day O'Connor (1930–) was born in El Paso, Texas, as the Depression strangled the U.S. and world economies. As a young woman, after being admitted to the bar in California she settled in Arizona, where she was appointed assistant attorney general in 1965. She then successfully campaigned for a seat in the state Senate. She had served for four years as a judge of the Superior Court of Maricopa County and for two years on the state Court of Appeals when, in 1981, a presidential appointment raised her from relative obscurity to the status of first woman associate justice of the U.S. Supreme Court.

Georgia O'Keeffe (1887–1986), a Wisconsin farm child, studied at the Art Institute of Chicago and the Art Students' League in New York as a young woman. She worked designing lace and embroidery patterns, then prepared to teach design, but her plans changed after some of her drawings were exhibited at Alfred Stieglitz's studio in 1916, without her prior knowledge. She married the great photographer in 1924. He pho-tographed her hundreds of times. When he died in 1946 she settled in New Mexico, which she had visited often. In 1944 she wrote to Eleanor Roosevelt, "It seems to me very important . . . that all men and women stand equal under the sky." She painted abstract images based on natural objects, and rural buildings, but is best known for precise close-ups of flowers and for crisp images of desert objects, painted in later years.

The wealthy parents of **Jacqueline Bouvier Kennedy Onassis** (1929–1994) separated when she was eight. An expert rider, she absorbed France's language and culture. At 21 she won a major *Vogue* magazine contest, partly by writing why she would have liked to know (her choices) Baudelaire, Wilde, and Diaghilev. As a young reporter, she interviewed Pat Nixon, wife of then Vice President Richard Nixon. Said her husband, President John F. Kennedy, in 1961 in France, where she was much admired, "I'm the man who accompanied Jackie." A fashion-setter who superbly restored White House interiors, she guarded family privacy and said, "If you bungle bringing up your children, whatever else you do well doesn't matter."

Canadian-born **Mary Pickford** (1893–1979) became a child actress after her father died and her mother took in theatrical boarders in Toronto. At 14 she starred in a Broadway play. By 1912 she had made 75 two-reel films. By signing with rival studios, she went from $40 a week in 1910 to $350,000 a film in 1917. That year, she portrayed *Rebecca of Sunnybrook Farm* and *The Little Princess*. In 1919 she founded United Artists with Douglas Fairbanks, D. W. Griffith, and Charlie Chaplin, and married Fairbanks. She played Pollyanna when she was 27. Unable to break away from child roles, she retired from acting at 40. When she formed a corporation, "her mother, Charlotte, was all the vice presidents." In 1936 she and Fairbanks divorced. Pickford and Chaplin sold United Artists in 1953.

Eleanor Roosevelt (1884–1962), orphaned at 10, was sent by a strict grandmother to a boarding school in England, where the French headmistress gave her affection and helped her gain confidence. At 34, she had six children and a dour mother-in-law—and discovered her husband Franklin Delano Roosevelt's affair with her social secretary during World War I. In 1921 FDR, then New York's governor, was stricken with polio. Eleanor became active in Democratic party organizing.

During his presidency (1932–1945), she made hundreds of visits like her famed coal-mine descent. In a 1933 interview she said, "I try to understand people" instead of getting angry. Twice U.S. Delegate to the United Nations, she drafted the Universal Declaration of Human Rights in 1948. A leading conservative Republican, Clare Boothe Luce, said of liberal Democrat Eleanor Roosevelt, "she did more than anyone else to comfort the needy and discomfit the powerful."

Helena Rubinstein (1882–1965), born in Poland to a prosperous family, studied medicine briefly, but on a 1902 trip to Australia, noting the harsh climate, she sent for a family recipe for face cream and began selling jars of it. She opened a beauty salon, and had others in London, Paris, and New York by 1915. After World War I she developed laboratories, factories, training schools, and a worldwide sales force. New products such as waterproof mascara emerged during a long rivalry with Elizabeth Arden. Short, plump, and unmadeover (as a "worker," she said, she was too busy for elaborate beauty routines), she filled five mansions with antiques and art, and still ran board meetings from her bed at 82.

Margaret Sanger (1883–1966) saw her worn-out mother of 11 die at 49. Helped by two older sisters, she worked at college and was a practical nurse and mother of three by 1910. Mr. Sanger had said she must marry him "now or never," so she reluctantly gave up studying to be a registered nurse. She left suburbia to nurse in New York City slums and promote workers' rights. In 1914 she began publishing *The Woman Rebel* and a "how-to" birth-control booklet. Her aim was economic and personal health: ". . . until woman [can] control birth . . . . she will remain the drudge that she is and her husband the slave that he is . . . as they . . . supply . . . cheap labor." Soon after her 5-year-old daughter died of pneumonia, she kept the first physician-staffed birth-control clinic open for 10 days—in Brooklyn. After divorcing, she married a millionaire in 1922. Decades of struggle formed Planned Parenthood (1942) and an international federation (1952). By 1960, U.S. women could buy birth-control pills.

Margaret Chase Smith (1897–1995) worked for many years before marrying. As a legislative aide, she was elected to the House of Representatives in 1940 to take her husband's place when he died. In 1949 she became the first woman elected senator. A conservative Republican (her assistant was a major general, and she earned high Air Force Reserve rank), she voted by conscience, not party. On June 1, 1950, her memorable "Declaration of Conscience" speech chided powerful Republican Sen. Joseph McCarthy for "selfish political exploitation of fear . . . and intolerance." The response to her courage prompted the interview query, "What if you woke up in the White House?" She jokingly replied, "I'd go straight to Mrs. Truman and apologize. Then I'd go home." She "retired" in 1973, teaching at colleges, writing for major periodicals, and publishing two books.

Gertrude Stein (1874–1946), from Alleghany, Pa., studied psychology and medicine at Radcliffe College and at Johns Hopkins University. Later, between World Wars I and II, as an experimental writer, she hosted a Paris salon with her longtime companion, Alice B. Toklas, that attracted a brilliant range of 20th-century European and U.S.-expatriate writers and artists.

Her fictional *Autobiography of Alice B. Toklas*, a best-seller, brought attention to her other works, such as *Three Lives, The Making of Americans, Tender Buttons,* and *Matisse, Picasso and Gertrude Stein.* This unconventional woman remarked, "Everybody knows if you are too careful you are so occupied in being careful that you are sure to stumble over something."

Harriet Beecher Stowe (1811–1896), a child of famed Calvinist preacher Lyman Beecher, had the renowned Catharine and Rev. Henry Ward Beecher among her seven siblings. After the family moved to raw Cincinnati, she married widowed Professor Stowe and promptly had six children, though she hated domestic chores. She managed to write long letters, but little else. Her baby died of cholera in 1849, but a girl was born before the 1850 Fugitive Slave Act's effects called forth *Uncle Tom's Cabin*. (She said it "wrote itself.") In a few 1852 days, 10,000 copies were sold. George Sand praised it. Queen Victoria and English writer on economics and social issues Harriet Martineau preferred her 1856 *Dred*. Despite sorrows (four of her children died young), Harriet wrote many more books—three nostalgic New England novels by 1869.

Harriet Tubman (1820–1913), born a slave in Maryland, labored as a field hand. Despite a head injury that made her "fall asleep" without warning, in 1849 she escaped to Philadelphia to avoid being sold to the Deep South after her owner died. In 1850 and 1851 she went back to Baltimore, guiding her sister's and her brother's families to freedom. Her parents also were aided to escape. In 10 years of dangerous trips, she led at least 300 slaves North, using the Underground Railroad. During the Civil War she was a cook, laundress, nurse, scout, and spy. In 1869 she and new husband Nelson Davies opened schools for "freemen." She later made a home for elderly ex-slaves in Auburn, N.Y., using money from book sales of her life story.

Diana Vreeland (1906–1989), born in Paris to English parents, was brought to the United States in 1914. As a girl, she traveled, read European literature in translation, and was at ballet school as much as at regular school. At 18 she married a banker. With their two children, they lived in Albany, N.Y., then in Paris until 1935. She was fashion editor at *Harper's Bazaar* 1937–1962. Her column suggested washing children's hair in champagne, but she insisted, "Money has nothing to do with style at all."*Vogue* editor until 1971, she became a special consultant to the Costume Institute of the Metropolitan Museum, creating sumptuous exhibits. "To evoke the imagination of the public is a wonderful thing if you can manage it," she mused.

Lillian Wald (1867–1940), born in Ohio to German immigrants, attended boarding school, studied nursing at New York Hospital, then nursed orphans. Leaving the Women's Medical College, in 1895 she began serving slum dwellers, with financial aid from the wealthy German-Jewish Loebs and Schiffs— and the Henry Street Settlement soon grew. At the time, Wald knew nothing of existing "settlements." With Florence Kelley, she founded the Child Labor Commission in 1904. Henry Street Settlement's 92 nurses made 200,000 visits in 1913; 3,000 people were in clubs and classes. (Wald valued music, art, and folktales, thanks to her grandfather.) With Jane Addams, she opposed U.S. entry into World War I. The nurses faced a deadly influenza epidemic in 1918. After 1924 Wald was usually ill, but Henry Street's services expanded during the Depression.

After college, **Barbara Walters** (1931–) became a television reporter. From 1961 onward, she progressed from being a writer to cohosting *The Today Show*. The first female network news evening anchor/"author" (1976), she also produced special programs and chaired *Not for Women Only*. Known for "aggressively" interviewing Sadat, Fidel Castro, and many others, she twice was one of *Harper's* top 10 Women of Accomplishment. In 1974 she was among *Time's* 200 Leaders of the Future. Gallup polls named her a "most admired" U.S. woman. Remarkably, she also was the single mother of two children. Being a parent, she once said, "is tough. If you just want a wonderful little creature to love, . . . get a puppy."

Edith Wharton (1862–1937), born in a fashionable townhouse in Manhattan, visited Italy, France, and Spain as a child. Educated by tutors, she published a book of poems at 16, married at 23, and wrote stories (published in two volumes). Settling in Europe in 1907, she enjoyed a friendship with Henry James. Her marriage (her husband was mentally unstable) ended in 1913. During World War I, she did charity and refugee work, raising funds for 600 Belgian children to flee the German invasion. Author of 20 novels and some nonfiction (travel, architecture, and gardens were among her subjects), she won Pulitzer prizes in 1921 and 1935. She feared that her writing might go out with "tufted furniture and gas chandeliers," but *The House of Mirth* (1905), *Ethan Frome* (1911), and *The Age of Innocence* (1920) still are widely read.

Oprah Winfrey (1954–) television host, producer, film actress, and mentor to girls and young women, lived with her mother as a child, but later her remarried father guided his daughter's education and personal development. After college in Nashville she became a local television reporter. "Luck is a matter of preparation meeting opportunity," she believes. She was magnificent in her first acting role, in the film version of Alice Walker's novel *The Color Purple.* Having gained a lot of weight to play the part, she since has shared with millions of women her efforts to banish excess weight. Said Maya Angelou of her, "She is an honest, hard-working woman who has . . . an unusual amount of caring and courage."